013

A CINEMATIC HISTORY of WAR & EPICS

www.raintreepublishers.co.uk
Visit our website to find out more information about
Raintree books.

To order:
☎ Phone 44 (0) 1865 888113
🖹 Send a fax to 44 (0) 1865 314091
💻 Visit the Raintree bookshop at
www.raintreepublishers.co.uk to browse our
catalogue and order online.

A CINEMATIC HISTORY OF WAR & EPICS
was produced by

David West 👥 Children's Books

7 Princeton Court
55 Felsham Road
London SW15 1AZ

Designer: Gary Jeffrey
Editor: Rowan Lawton, Kate Newport
Picture Research: Gail Bushnell

First published in Great Britain by
Raintree, Halley Court, Jordan Hill, Oxford OX2
8EJ, part of Harcourt Education. Raintree is a
registered trademark of Harcourt Education Ltd.

08 07 06 05
10 9 8 7 6 5 4 3 2 1

ISBN 1 844 21085 5

British Library Cataloguing in Publication Data

Wilshin, Mark
A cinematic history of war and epics
1.War films - History and criticism -Juvenile
   literature
2.Epic films - History and criticism -Juvenile
   literature
I.Title
                  791.4'3658

Printed and bound in China

PHOTO CREDITS :

Abbreviations: t-top, m-middle, b-bottom, r-right,
l-left, c-centre.

cover, t, DE LAURENTISS / MOSFILM / THE KOBAL COLLECTION, c,
WARNER BROS. / THE KOBAL COLLECTION / BAILEY, ALEX, r, REPBULIC /
THE KOBAL COLLECTION; 3, Photo By EVERETT COLLECTION / REX
FEATURES; 4l, Photo By EVERETT COLLECTION / REX FEATURES, 4c, Photo
By C.WARNER BR/EVERETT / REX FEATURES; 5, Photo By REX FEATURES; 6t,
MGM / THE KOBAL COLLECTION, 6l, Photo By REX FEATURES, 6r,
PARAMOUNT / THE KOBAL COLLECTION; 7t, MGM / THE KOBAL
COLLECTION, 7l, Photo By C.DREAMWRKS/EVERETT / REX FEATURES, 7r,
Photo By C.WARNER BR/EVERETT / REX FEATURES; 8t, MOSFILMS / THE
KOBAL COLLECTION, 8b, ALLIED ARTISTS / THE KOBAL COLLECTION, 9t,
Photo By C.20THC.FOX/EVERETT / REX FEATURES, 9l, ORION/WARNER
BROS / THE KOBAL COLLECTION , 9r, Photo By REX FEATURES; 10t, 10b,
Photo By EVERETT COLLECTION / REX FEATURES, 11l, Photo By
C.PARAMOUNT/EVERETT / REX FEATURES, 11r, Photo By REX FEATURES;
12l, Photo By EVERETT COLLECTION / REX FEATURES, 12b, GOSKINO / THE
KOBAL COLLECTION, 12r, TOMSON FILMS/CHINA FILM/BEIJING / THE
KOBAL COLLECTION; 13t, COLUMBIA/SONY / THE KOBAL COLLECTION /
CHUEN, CHAN KAM, 13b, BEIJING NEW PICTURE/ELITE GROUP / THE
KOBAL COLLECTION; 14t, Photo By SNAP / REX FEATURES, 14l,
SELZNICK/MGM / THE KOBAL COLLECTION, 24r, Photo By SNAP / REX
FEATURES; 15t, MGM / THE KOBAL COLLECTION, 15c, Photo By EVERETT
COLLECTION / REX FEATURES, 15b, COLUMBIA TRISTAR / THE KOBAL
COLLECTION / COOPER, ANDREW; 16t, Photo By SNAP / REX FEATURES.
16l, Photo By EVERETT COLLECTION / REX, 16r, UNITED ARTISTS / THE
KOBAL COLLECTION; 17t, Photo By EVERETT COLLECTION / REX, 17b,
RAFFORD FILMS/NORSTAR ENT / THE KOBAL COLLECTION; 18r, MGM /
THE KOBAL COLLECTION, 18l, 20TH CENTURY FOX / THE KOBAL
COLLECTION, 18b, Photo By REX FEATURES; 19t, Photo By
C.20THC.FOX/EVERETT / REX FEATURES, 19c, Photo By REX FEATURES, 19b,
Photo By REX FEATURES; 20t, RKO / THE KOBAL COLLECTION, 20b, Photo
By EVERETT COLLECTION / REX FEATURES, 20/21c, Photo By EVERETT
COLLECTION / REX FEATURES; 21t, Photo By EVERETT COLLECTION / REX
FEATURES, 21b, Photo By SNAP / REX FEATURES; 22t, Photo By EVERETT
COLLECTION / REX FEATURES, 22r, MIRISCH/UNITED ARTISTS / THE
KOBAL COLLECTION 22l, Photo By EVERETT COLLECTION / REX
FEATURES; 23t, PRODUZIONE DE SICA / THE KOBAL COLLECTION, 23b,
Photo By EVERETT COLLECTION / REX FEATURES; 24t, OLYMPIA-FILM /
THE KOBAL COLLECTION, 24b,
PEGASO/ITALNOLEGGIO/PRAESIDENS/EICHBERG / THE KOBAL
COLLECTION; 25l, FILMS ALEPH/HISTORIA / THE KOBAL COLLECTION,
25r, MELAMPO CINEMATOGRAFICA / THE KOBAL COLLECTION / STRIZZI,
SERGIO, 25b, UNIVERSAL / THE KOBAL COLLECTION / JAMES, DAVID; 26r,
Photo By C. ORION/EVERETT / REX FEATURES, 26l, Photo By SNAP / REX
FEATURES, 26b, Photo By C.U.A./EVERETT / REX FEATURES; 27t, Photo By
C.PARAMOUNT/EVERETT / REX FEATURES, 27c, Photo By
C.COLUMBIA/EVERETT / REX FEATURES, 27b, Photo By
C.MIRAMAX/EVERETT / REX FEATURES; 28t, Photo By EVERETT
COLLECTION / REX FEATURES, 28b, C.MIRAMAX/EVERETT / REX
FEATURES; 29t, Photo By SIPA PRESS / REX FEATURES, 29b, Photo By
EVERETT COLLECTION / REX FEATURES; 30t, Photo By EVERETT
COLLECTION / REX FEATURES, 30l, LUCASFILM LTD/PARAMOUNT / THE
KOBAL COLLECTION, 30b, MGM / THE KOBAL COLLECTION

Every effort has been made to contact copyright
holders of any material reproduced in this book.
Any omissions will be rectified in subsequent
printings if notice is given to the publishers.

*An explanation of difficult words can be
found in the glossary on page 31.*

A CINEMATIC HISTORY of WAR & EPICS

MARK WILSHIN

Raintree

CONTENTS

INTRODUCTION

With tales of romance, royalty and revenge in faraway lands and past times, the screen epic is a lavish spectacle of big sets, big stars and big budgets. Beginning in Italy in the era of silent films with the wars and intrigues of Ancient Rome, the epic came to a temporary close with the hugely extravagant Cleopatra (1963) until its recent revival, with sword and sandal sagas and computer-generated epics. While the epic often uses history and war as a dramatic backdrop for stories of heroism and passion, the war film is centred round the bloody battlefields and muddy trenches of the frontline. From the American Civil War (1861–1865) to the Vietnam War (1954–1975), cinema screens have been bombarded with arrows, bombs, and gas attacks, vividly depicting the terror and the tragedy of our world at war.

SWORDS AND SANDALS

Thrilling audiences with gladiators and chariot races, the sword and sandal epic triumphed during the 1950s, and recently became popular again with its heroic battles and grisly fights.

BIBLE STUDIES

While Hollywood skimped on sword and sandal epics during the silent era, the **genre** was extremely popular in Italy, with films like *Cabiria* (1914) and *Quo Vadis?* (1912) bringing spectacular battles and vast processions to life. In the 1950s, Hollywood made its own epics based on the Bible, with films such as *The Robe* (1953), the first to capture epic grandeur in widescreen.

BEN HUR (1925)

The most expensive silent movie ever made, Ben Hur contains scenes in colour, as well as spectacular sea battles and chariot races.

SAMSON AND DELILAH (1949)

Samson and Delilah is a biblical epic, depicting Samson's attempts to free the Jews from slavery under the Philistines. Betrayed by the beautiful Delilah, Samson is weakened when she cuts off his hair.

SPARTACUS (1960)

A dark epic about freedom, courage, and leadership, director Stanley Kubrick's Spartacus depicts an uprising of slaves led by the trained gladiator Spartacus against the brutal **Roman Empire.**

CECIL B. DEMILLE

The iconic Hollywood director Cecil B. DeMille shot to fame with comedies like Don't Change Your Husband *(1919), before concentrating on epic spectacles like* The Ten Commandments *(1923) and* The King of Kings *(1927).*

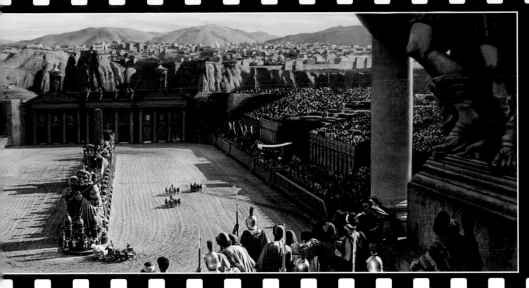

BEN HUR (1959)

Ben Hur *is an epic tale of revenge. The 1959 version starred Charlton Heston as the legendary hero, a wealthy Jewish merchant betrayed by a friend, sold into slavery and his family murdered. Winning eleven Academy Awards,* Ben Hur *saved MGM Studios from bankruptcy, stunning audiences with its incredible chariot races.*

BLOOD ON THE SAND

The monumental drama *Cleopatra* (1963), starring Elizabeth Taylor, had a cast of thousands. The film brought a swift end to the sword and sandals epic, as it bankrupted the 20th Century Fox film studio. Recently, tunic-wearing warriors have fought their way back on to the silver screen with films like *Gladiator* (2000) and *Troy* (2004), which traces the epic war between the Greeks and the Trojans.

GLADIATOR (2000)

Set in the world of Roman politics, the award-winning Gladiator *shows the Roman General Maximus in his quest for revenge against the Emperor, who murdered his family and made him a slave.*

ALEXANDER (2004)

Based on historical fact, Alexander *follows the warrior Alexander the Great in his quest to conquer the world, when his friend Hephaestion is killed.*

MEDIEVAL WARS

Armed for battle with lances and pikes, knights on horseback, with their codes of honour, have shocked audiences with bloody and brutal warfare.

CHARLTON HESTON

Having launched his acting career on the stage and television, Heston made his cinematic breakthrough as a circus director in The Greatest Show on Earth *(1952). He became a Hollywood star in* The Ten Commandments *(1956) and won an Oscar for* Ben Hur *(1959).*

CHIVALRY

Combining mythology and history, the national epic portrays the most important events in a country's history. Based on a German poem, Fritz Lang's *Die Nibelungen* (1924) depicts the dragon-slaying folk hero Siegfried, while Eisenstein's *Ivan the Terrible* (1945) portrays the violent battles that united Russia. The medieval epic sometimes comments on contemporary issues, such as Laurence Olivier's *Henry the Fifth* (1944), filmed to encourage the Allied soldiers during World War II (1939–1945), with its depiction of **patriotic** battles.

ALEXANDER NEVSKY (1938)

With a stunning battle scene on a frozen lake, Alexander Nevsky shows a Russian prince in the 13th century, raising an army to defend Russia against invasion.

EL CID (1961)

Full of battles and sieges, El Cid stars Charlton Heston as the knight Rodrigo, and Sophia Loren as his ill-fated lover Jimena. Armed with the knightly virtues of mercy and self-sacrifice, El Cid unites Christians and **Moors** *in their quest to defend Spain from invasion.*

BRAVEHEART (1995)

Directed by and starring Mel Gibson, Braveheart *is loosely based on the legend of Scottish folk hero William Wallace, who joined forces with Robert the Bruce in the 13th century to free Scotland from English occupation. Winning five Academy awards,* Braveheart *depicts the brutality of war in the medieval era with its violent and bloody battle scenes.*

BLOOD BATHS

Shakespeare plays have also been used to depict the violence of medieval times, with Japanese adaptations of <u>Macbeth</u> and <u>King Lear</u> in Kurosawa's epic films *Throne of Blood* (1957) and *Ran* (1985). French cinema exposes the treachery of the French court in *La Reine Margot* (1994), with its bloody portrait of a religious massacre in 1572, when thousands of Protestants were killed by Catholics.

KING ARTHUR (2004)

Set in the lawless and godless Britain of the **Dark Ages**, King Arthur *follows Arthur and his band of barbaric knights as they defend their homeland from Saxon invasion in epic blood-drenched battles.*

EXCALIBUR (1981)

Following the fate of the magical sword from its release from the stone by Arthur to its return to the water, Excalibur *combines the mystical elements of the kingdom of Camelot, and the Lady of the Lake, with grisly deaths and violent battles.*

CHARGE!

Full of cavalry charges, cannon fire and colonial wars, the military epic focuses on the spectacle of war, with vast battlefields, huge explosions and heroic deeds.

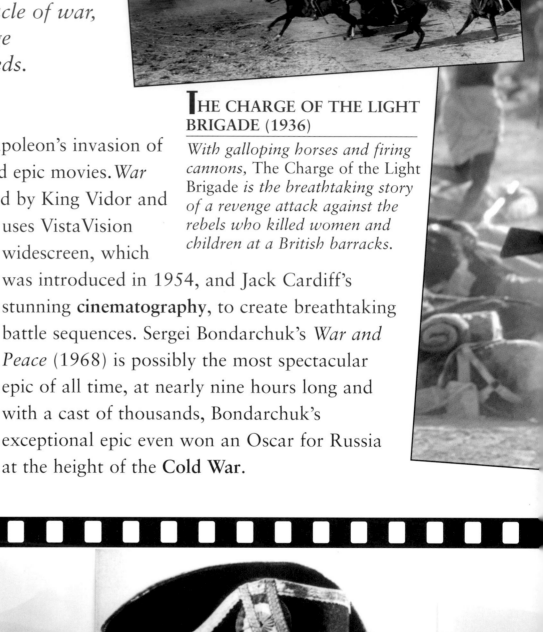

WAR AND PEACE

Leo Tolstoy's novel about Napoleon's invasion of Russia has inspired two grand epic movies. *War and Peace* (1956) was directed by King Vidor and uses VistaVision widescreen, which was introduced in 1954, and Jack Cardiff's stunning **cinematography**, to create breathtaking battle sequences. Sergei Bondarchuk's *War and Peace* (1968) is possibly the most spectacular epic of all time, at nearly nine hours long and with a cast of thousands, Bondarchuk's exceptional epic even won an Oscar for Russia at the height of the **Cold War**.

ABEL GANCE

Gance started his career as an actor and scriptwriter. Success came with his experimental anti-war film J'accuse! *(1919). With real-life footage of World War I (1914–1918), it documents the horrors of war.*

THE CHARGE OF THE LIGHT BRIGADE (1936)

With galloping horses and firing cannons, The Charge of the Light Brigade *is the breathtaking story of a revenge attack against the rebels who killed women and children at a British barracks.*

THE FOUR FEATHERS (2002)

The fifth film of A.E.W. Mason's novel, The Four Feathers examines ideas of bravery and honour, as an officer receives white feathers, symbolizing cowardice, when he resigns before a battle.

DEATH AND GLORY

After *War and Peace* (1968), Bondarchuk directed *Waterloo* (1970), a recreation of the battle between Napoleon and the Duke of Wellington. Focusing on the political intrigues of war, Stanley Kubrick's *Barry Lyndon* (1975) was filmed with special camera lenses that made the battlefields of Europe look like classical paintings. Colonial wars in Africa and India are also recreated in films like *The Lives of a Bengal Lancer* (1935) and *Zulu* (1964).

THE LAST SAMURAI (2003)

In a Japan caught between tradition and modernity, The Last Samurai stars Tom Cruise as a drunken soldier, recruited by the Emperor to train the Japanese army to use rifles. When he is captured by Samurai, he learns to respect Samurai culture, deciding to take up the sword himself.

NAPOLEON (1927)

Napoleon is a six-hour epic, documenting the life of Napoleon, from boyhood to his invasion of Italy. He is shown to be both selfish and heroic. Using experimental techniques, director Abel Gance projected the final spectacular battle scenes on to three screens, creating vast battlefields in widescreen and complex combinations of three separate images. The film's use of widescreen was 30 years ahead of its time and influenced generations of film directors.

EASTERN EPICS

Creating revolutionary epics and spectacular martial arts movies, Russia and China have greatly contributed to the history of cinema, with movies that blend poetry and politics together.

MONTAGE THEORY

Montage is the editing of single shots into a meaningful sequence. Using the same shot of an actor, different shots of soup, and a child's coffin, filmmaker Kuleshov showed how montage creates meaning, when viewers thought the actor's emotions changed in every shot.

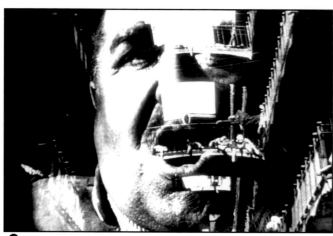

STRIKE! (1925)

Depicting events leading to the Russian Revolution, Eisenstein's debut film focuses on the massacre of factory workers by soldiers.

REVOLUTIONS

Inspired by the Russian Revolution of 1917, the director Eisenstein recreated the uprising in *October* (1927), and David Lean filmed an epic about a man caught up in the revolution in *Dr Zhivago* (1965). The typically epic themes of suffering and betrayal have also been explored in films about the Chinese Cultural Revolution, such as *Farewell My Concubine* (1993).

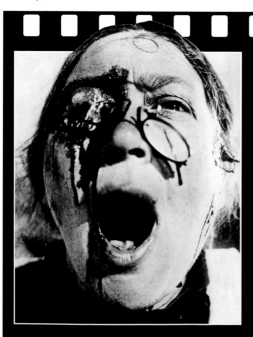

BATTLESHIP POTEMKIN (1925)

Based on the historical events of 1905, Battleship Potemkin *portrays the sailors' uprising when they are served disgusting, maggot-infested meat. When those who refuse to eat are lined up in front of a firing squad, the sailors rebel and revolution spreads to the port of Odessa. Battleship Potemkin contains a famous massacre scene of robotic soldiers murdering innocent people on the Odessa steps. The film is arguably Eisenstein's revolutionary masterpiece.*

FAREWELL MY CONCUBINE (1993)

Set during China's **Cultural Revolution**, the film follows two stars of the Peking Opera from their brutal school days to the revolution, when love, betrayal and death drive them apart.

CROUCHING TIGER HIDDEN DRAGON (2000)

Gliding through the air, running up walls and gracefully fighting in the tops of bamboo trees, the Oscar-winning Crouching Tiger Hidden Dragon *is a martial arts epic of repressed love and noble swordsmen.*

ANG LEE

Born in Taiwan, Ang Lee examined Taiwanese culture and family conflict in The Wedding Banquet *(1993) and* Eat Drink Man Woman *(1994) before making his name in Hollywood with stifled passions in* Sense and Sensibility *(1995).*

EASTERN PROMISE

Banned by the Chinese government in the 1930s, the 'wuxia' or Chinese martial arts film has been popular for decades in Asia, but first arrived in the West with Ang Lee's *Crouching Tiger Hidden Dragon* (2000). Mixing supernatural powers with amazing swordplay, the wuxia film has an epic style with its spectacular snow-capped mountains, bamboo forests and black lakes. While Zhang Yimou's film *House of Flying Daggers* (2004) is a love story, *Hero* (2002) has more of a political focus.

HERO (2002)

The most expensive film ever made in Chinese cinema, Hero *offers several different stories explaining how an unnamed assassin defeated the king's three greatest enemies.*

STARS AND STRIPES

With smoking cannons and rifles, the American Civil War was fought from 1861 to 1865 between the Yankees of the North and the Dixies in the South.

YANKEES AND DIXIES

While often the subject of western adventures in films like *Virginia City* (1940) and *Fort Apache* (1948), the American Civil War has also become the setting of national epics, like D.W. Griffith's controversial film, *The Birth of a Nation* (1915). Focusing on a divided America, *The Battle of Gettysburg* (1913) follows a woman torn between her Yankee sweetheart and her Dixie brother, while films like *Secret Service* (1919) and *A Southern Yankee* (1948) are spy tales.

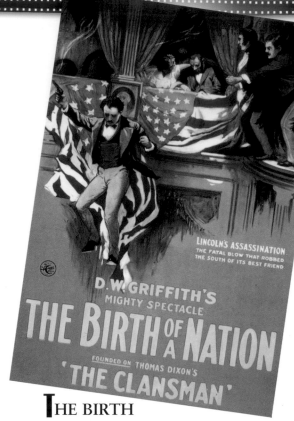

THE BIRTH OF A NATION (1915)

*Making over U.S.$10 million, The Birth of a Nation was the highest earning silent film. But it caused controversy with its racist story of the **Ku Klux Klan** freeing the South from the evil Yankees and sparked a revival of the Klan.*

GONE WITH THE WIND (1939)

At almost four hours, Gone with the Wind is an epic tale of survival during the Civil War, as Southern belle Scarlett battles starvation and unhappy marriages to save her home.

D.W. GRIFFITH

This American film director is famous for his experiments with film editing techniques. After The Birth of a Nation *(1915), Griffith was accused of racism, leading him to make* Intolerance *(1916), a film about human prejudice.*

THE RED BADGE OF COURAGE (1951)

Starring American war hero Audie Murphy, John Huston's The Red Badge of Courage *follows a young volunteer soldier who deserts during his first battle but returns to carry the flag after encountering dying soldiers.*

BATTLE WEARY

With Native Americans often portrayed as villains in western-style war films like *She Wore a Yellow Ribbon* (1949), the spectacular epic *Dances with Wolves* (1990) paints a more positive portrait, when a heroic cavalry officer sent to a remote outpost gives up his position to join a tribe of Dakota Indians. While *Gettysburg* (1993) is an epic recreation of the real three day battle, *Cold Mountain* (2003) follows a wounded and disillusioned Southern deserter on his perilous journey home to his sweetheart.

MAJOR DUNDEE (1965)

A Civil War western, Major Dundee *stars Charlton Heston as a disgraced captain in charge of a group of prisoners of war, on a mission to rescue soldiers from Apache Indians.*

THE PATRIOT (2000)

Set in South Carolina, The Patriot *depicts a former soldier drawn into the American War of Independence when his son is killed by a British colonel.*

GLORY (1989)

Based on the life of Colonel Robert G. Shaw, Glory *depicts the first battalion of the American Civil War to be made up entirely of black soldiers. Under the command of the heroic officer Shaw, the freed slaves prove their honour and bravery, fighting for the Union army. Exposing the grim realities of war,* Glory *conveys the courage of ordinary soldiers fighting the enemy through hazardous battles.*

WORLD WAR I

*The war to end all wars, World War I saw death on a massive scale, as soldiers starved in muddy trenches before facing shell-fire in **no man's land.***

TERROR OF THE TRENCHES

With haunting scenes of dead soldiers, Abel Gance's *J'accuse* (1919) was one of the first anti-war films, using real footage of French battlefields to depict the horrors of trench warfare. Similarly exposing the stupidity of war, *The Four Horsemen of the Apocalypse* (1921) features a French soldier facing his German brother-in-law on the battlefield. Other films like *Wings* (1927) tried to capture the bravery and heroism of fighter pilots.

ALL QUIET ON THE WESTERN FRONT (1930)

Adapted from E.M. Remarque's famous anti-war novel, All Quiet on the Western Front *depicts the fear and disillusionment of a German soldier confronted with the futility of war and the tragic waste of human life.*

SERGEANT YORK (1941)

Based on the life of an American World War I soldier, Sergeant York *is a sniper, who single-handedly captures over one hundred Germans using his turkey shooting strategy.*

REMEMBERANCE

The tragedy and senselessness of war was revisited in the 1930s as a second world war loomed. G.W. Pabst called for tolerance in his bleak anti-war film *Westfront 18* (1930) while Renoir's *La Grande Illusion* (1937) challenged the illusion that war solves everything. Later films took a different approach to the war, with Richard Attenborough's musical *Oh What a Lovely War!* (1969) and *Gallipoli* (1981), focusing on Australian troops fighting in Turkey.

LAWRENCE OF ARABIA (1962)

Loosely based on the life of T.E. Lawrence, Lawrence of Arabia *is a stunning widescreen epic of heat-hazed deserts and dramatic battles as a British lieutenant leads the Arabs in their fight against the Turks.*

DAVID LEAN

David Lean shot to fame with his romance film Brief Encounter *(1945). After winning an Oscar for* The Bridge on the River Kwai *(1957), Lean made his stunning epics* Lawrence of Arabia *(1962) and* Doctor Zhivago *(1965).*

PATHS OF GLORY (1957)

Directed by Stanley Kubrick, Paths of Glory *follows Colonel Dax and his regiment in the French trenches, sent on a suicide mission by a glory-seeking General to capture a well-defended hill. Driven back by shells and bullets, three of the rebellious survivors are tried for cowardice. Banned in France for its portrait of the French military,* Paths of Glory *paints a bleak picture of the horror of the trenches and the haunting eeriness of no man's land.*

REGENERATION (1997)

With its brutal depiction of life in the trenches, Regeneration *is centred round the shell-shocked war poets Wilfred Owen and Siegfried Sassoon, who meet at a military hospital in Scotland, where they are made well enough to return to the front.*

WORLD WAR II

With military air combat, underwater torpedoes and fighting behind enemy lines, cinema has captured the heroic and tragic battles of World War II on land, air, and sea.

CALL TO ARMS

Sea battles have been the subject of films like *In Which We Serve* (1942) and *Action in the North Atlantic* (1943), depicting a submarine attack on an American convoy. Air attacks were recreated in *The Battle of Britain* (1969) and *The Dam Busters* (1954), where Britain tests its newly invented bouncing bombs. *A Bridge Too Far* (1977) depicts the failed attempt to end the war quickly by capturing three important bridges.

BATAAN (1943)

Made during the war as a tribute to American soldiers, Bataan depicts a platoon making one last stand against the invading Japanese army in the jungle.

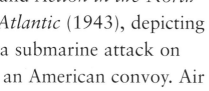

DARRYL F. ZANUCK *presents*

TWELVE O'CLOCK HIGH

Starring

GREGORY PECK

HUGH MARLOWE · GARY MERRILL · MILLARD MITCHELL · DEAN JAGGER · ROBERT ARTHUR · PAUL STEWART · JOHN KELLOGG · BOB PATTEN

PRODUCED BY DARRYL F. ZANUCK · DIRECTED BY HENRY KING

TWELVE O'CLOCK HIGH (1949)

Twelve O'Clock High uses real combat footage to show daredevil sky battles. The film also examines the psychological cost to pilots on dangerous daylight bombing missions.

THE GOOD FIGHT

Important battles like the Normandy landings are recreated in films such as *The Longest Day* (1962). The brutal Battle of Stalingrad is seen through German eyes in *Stalingrad* (1993), while ferocious fighting between American troops and the Japanese is recreated in *Guadalcanal Diary* (1943) and *The Thin Red Line* (1998).

TORA! TORA! TORA! (1970)

Directed by both Japanese and American directors, Tora! Tora! Tora! depicts Japan's surprise attack on Pearl Harbour.

STEVEN SPIELBERG

Making his film debut with Duel *(1971), Spielberg has directed action-packed adventures like* Jaws *(1975), sci-fi flicks like E.T. (1982), as well as poignant films about war such as* Empire of the Sun *(1987) and Saving Private Ryan (1998).*

SAVING PRIVATE RYAN (1998)

Loosely based on the true story of the Niland brothers, Saving Private Ryan follows a platoon of American soldiers through the Normandy beach landings, in their mission to save Private Ryan. Withdrawn from combat, because his three brothers have already been killed in the war, Private Ryan is tracked down by Captain Miller and his unit, as they take up their dangerous mission behind enemy lines. With its shaky handheld camera and bleak colours, Saving Private Ryan paints a gritty, realistic picture of the Normandy invasion at Omaha beach.

DAS BOOT (1981)

A grimly realistic portrait of terrified soldiers in a claustrophobic submarine, Das Boot shows World War II combat from the German point of view, as they battle underwater U-boats and confront their own doubts.

ENEMY AT THE GATES (2001)

Set during the decisive Battle of Stalingrad in 1942, Enemy at the Gates focuses on the real-life Russian sniper Vassili Zaitsev. Picking off German officers one by one, the sniper is drawn into a terrifying game with Germany's best gunman.

OCCUPATION AND RESISTANCE

While countries at war made fighting films to boost soldiers' morale, conquered countries, like France and Eastern Europe showed the war of occupation and resistance.

OCCUPIED

Made during the Nazi occupation, *The Raven* (1942) exposes the atmosphere of suspicion and spying in conquered France, as poison pen letters reveal a small town's secrets. Based on a resistance novel, *Le Silence de la Mer* (1947) captures the spirit of occupation and resistance, as a French uncle and niece coldly endure a German officer living in their home.

THIS LAND IS MINE (1943)

Fleeing to the U.S. in 1941, Jean Renoir directed this anti-Nazi film about life in occupied France. While some people collaborate with the Nazis for money or survival, a teacher decides to make a stand.

ROMAN POLANSKI

Born in 1933 to Polish parents, Roman Polanski survived the war, but his mother died in a concentration camp. After successes like Rosemary's Baby *(1968), Polanski returned to Poland to make* The Pianist *(2002).*

LACOMBE LUCIEN (1974)

Causing great controversy in France, Lacombe Lucien *was the first film to have a collaborator as its main character. Rejected by the Resistance, Lucien accidentally becomes involved with the German secret police.*

THE PIANIST (2002)

Based on an autobiography, The Pianist *is the story of a Jewish musician, who survives the war by hiding in the ruins of Warsaw in Poland. Dependent on the kindness and courage of others, the pianist is even helped by a German soldier.*

THE UNDERGROUND

The Shop on Main Street (1965) follows an assistant in a button shop, who must risk his own life to hide an old Jewish woman from the Nazis. Some films, like *Lucie Aubrac* (1997) focus on the heroism of the French resistance, with a woman outwitting the Nazi police to save her husband. Others such as *Army in the Shadows* (1969) reveal the everyday actions and bravery of civilians in wartime.

CHARLOTTE GRAY (2001)

Based on the novel by Sebastian Faulks, Charlotte Gray *follows a Scottish woman who becomes a British spy when her lover is shot down. Parachuted into France, she goes undercover, passing messages to the French resistance.*

AU REVOIR, LES ENFANTS (1987)

Set in a Catholic boarding school in Nazi-occupied France, Au Revoir, les Enfants *depicts the growing friendship between Julien, a Catholic boy, and Jean, a Jewish boy in hiding. Loosely based on director Louis Malle's own experiences at boarding school during World War II, the film shows both those who collaborated with the Germans and the priests who risked their lives to help those persecuted.*

TRIALS OF WAR

Rather than focus on the heroic soldiers and spies of traditional war movies, these films show prisoners of war trying to escape, and ordinary people struggling to rebuild their shattered lives.

ESCAPISM

Tunnelling their way out or disguised as German soldiers, prisoners of war have become the heroes of escape films like *The Colditz Story* (1955) and *Stalag 17* (1953). David Lean's *The Bridge on the River Kwai* (1957) focuses on a British officer's attempt to outdo the Japanese commanders by building a railway bridge. Films like *Paradise Road* (1997) and *To End all Wars* (2001) show the harsh brutality of prison life, as people do what they can to survive.

THE GREAT ESCAPE (1963)

Inspired by an escape from the highest security prison camp Stalag Luft III, The Great Escape shows the secret digging of a tunnel and Steve McQueen's famous motorcycle chase.

EMPIRE OF THE SUN (1987)

Based on the life of novelist J.G. Ballard, Empire of the Sun *depicts the experiences of a young boy in a Japanese prisoner of war camp. Separated from his parents, the boy must survive the war alone.*

THE STORY OF G.I. JOE (1945)

Centred round a popular war journalist, Ernie Pyle, The Story of G.I. Joe depicts his interviews with an American infantry unit, fighting its way from North Africa to Rome. Accompanying them in their bloody Italian campaign, the journalist learns the true nature of war, through the commanding officer and his soldiers. Focusing on the soldiers' daily lives rather than heroic battles, The Story of G.I. Joe shows their miserable, muddy living conditions as well as the exhaustion, fear and frustration of being a soldier.

THE BICYCLE THIEF (1948)

Using amateur actors and filmed on location in Italy, The Bicycle Thief follows a father and son as they desperately search Rome for a stolen bicycle. Focusing on the terrible poverty and hardship after the war, Vittorio De Sica's masterpiece depicts the human struggle to regain dignity.

WILLIAM WYLER

Serving as a major in the U.S. Air Corps, William Wyler continued to direct during the war, filming the documentaries The Memphis Belle *(1944) and* The Fighting Lady *(1944). Wyler also made* Mrs Miniver *(1942), about an English family getting used to wartime life.*

LIBERATION AND TRAUMA

As World War II ended, films focused on problems of liberation and rebuilding. Italian director Roberto Rossellini's realistic film *Paisan* (1946) depicts the harsh conditions after the war. *Germany Year Zero* (1948) shows a boy looking through the rubble of Berlin to find food. German and Japanese filmmakers also tried to come to terms with the war in *The Murderers Are Among Us* (1946) and *The Grave of the Fireflies* (1988).

THE BEST YEARS OF OUR LIVES (1946)

Depicting the homecoming of three soldiers to their quiet town in America, William Wyler's film, The Best Years of Our Lives, *concentrates on the joys and hardships of life after the war, as the men deal with disability and unemployment.*

NAZISM AND THE HOLOCAUST

Under the dictator Adolf Hitler, Nazi Germany murdered 12 to 26 million people. By killing Jews, **communists**, gypsies and homosexuals, the Nazis tried to declare themselves a master race.

IMAGES OF POWER

Using cinema as a powerful **propaganda** tool, Hitler's Germany made films like *Hitlerjunge Quex* (1933), glorifying Nazi heroes, as well as anti-Jewish films like *Jud Süß* (1940) and *Der Ewige Jude* (1940), depicting the Jews as scheming money-grabbers. Filmmaker Leni Riefenstahl made documentaries glorifying Nazi Germany, like *Olympia* (1938) and *Triumph of the Will* (1934), demonstrating the power of Germany's army at the 1934 Nazi rally in Nuremberg. Post-war films about Nazis, like *The Night Porter* (1974) focus on the extravagant and power-hungry nature of Nazism.

OLYMPIA (1938)

Commissioned as a propaganda piece by Adolf Hitler, Olympia is a documentary about the 1936 Olympics in Berlin, which gives a dazzling portrait of superhuman athletes, using groundbreaking editing techniques and camera angles.

THE DAMNED (1969)

Luchino Visconti's dark masterpiece depicts Germany's descent into corruption, as a wealthy German family is torn apart by greed and ambition.

LENI RIEFENSTAL

A documentary filmmaker in Hitler's Germany, Riefenstahl made propaganda films for the Nazi Party, such as Olympia *(1938) and* Triumph of the Will *(1934). Criticized for her films glorifying Nazi Germany, Riefenstahl is also highly regarded for her beautiful images of the human body.*

la fin du voyage.

FILMING THE UNTHINKABLE

Bearing witness to the millions who died at the hands of the Nazis, films about the **Holocaust** have attempted to depict the horrors of the extermination camps. Documentaries like *Shoah* (1985) and *Night and Fog* (1955) expose inhumanity, while Marcel Ophüls' *The Sorrow and the Pity* (1969) explores France's collaboration with Nazi Germany. Feature films like *The Last Stage* (1948) and *Kapò* (1959) recreate the prisoners' daily struggle to survive.

SHOAH (1985)

Meaning 'catastrophe' in Hebrew, Shoah is a monumental documentary made up of interviews with Holocaust survivors, former Nazis and local eye-witnesses. Running for nearly ten hours, Shoah slowly builds up a picture of the Holocaust from the stories of many of those involved, from the victims to the perpetrators.

LIFE IS BEAUTIFUL (1997)

Mixing the Holocaust with comedy, Life is Beautiful depicts a father's attempt to keep the horrors of the concentration camp away from his son, as he pretends it is just an elaborate game to win a real tank.

SCHINDLER'S LIST (1993)

Filmed in black and white, Schindler's List follows a German businessman, who employs cheap Jewish labour to work in his factory. When some of his workers are deported to a concentration camp, Oskar Schindler decides to get them back, creating a list to save the lives of nearly 1,200 Jews. Winning seven Academy Awards®, Schindler's List depicts the horrific brutality of the concentration camps and the Jewish ghettos.

THE VIETNAM MOVIE

Deeply scarred by the Vietnam War (1967–1975), American filmmakers recreated the nightmare of napalm gas attacks and jungle fighting, to question the human cost of war.

TO HELL AND BACK

While John Wayne's *The Green Berets* (1968), with its cowboy heroes and evil enemies, was a pro-war film to boost American troops, most films after the Vietnam War depict the brutality and inhumanity of the war. Oliver Stone's *Heaven and Earth* (1993) looks at the war from the viewpoint of a Vietnamese girl trying to survive.

OLIVER STONE

Stone has directed films such as JFK *(1991) and* Alexander *(2004). He made a trilogy of films about the Vietnam War:* Platoon *(1986),* Born on the Fourth of July *(1989), and* Heaven and Earth *(1993).*

PLATOON (1986)

Based on director Oliver Stone's experiences of the Vietnam War, Platoon *is a touching anti-war film, following a new recruit as war changes him from a naïve soldier into a brutal killer.*

FULL METAL JACKET (1987)

Filmed entirely in the United Kingdom, Stanley Kubrick's Full Metal Jacket *follows a unit of recruits from their military training with a cruel sergeant, to combat in Vietnam, where they discover the ability to kill.*

HAMBURGER HILL (1987)

Based on the nine day battle which turned soldiers into meat, Hamburger Hill *is a grimly realistic portrait of war, as a platoon of soldiers risk their lives to capture a heavily guarded hill.*

CASUALTIES OF WAR (1989)

Based on a true story, Brian De Palma's Casualties of War *gives a violent depiction of the inhumanity of war, as an American marine brings his fellow soldiers to justice for brutally beating and murdering a Vietnamese girl.*

The Deer Hunter (1978) paints a haunting picture of three soldiers warped by their harrowing experiences in a prison camp. The trauma of returning home is also the focus of films like *Birdy* (1984) and *Born on the Fourth of July* (1989), where a paralysed veteran becomes an anti-war protestor.

APOCALYPSE NOW (1979)

Inspired by Joseph Conrad's novel <u>Heart of Darkness</u>, Apocalypse Now *follows Captain Willard on a mission up river to kill Colonel Kurtz. As he journeys through the jungle, witnessing the horrors and madness of war, the soldier begins to question his mission. Notorious for its production problems and massive over spending, Francis Ford Coppola's film depicts the nightmare of war as a man searches the darkest depths of his own soul.*

THE QUIET AMERICAN (2002)

Adapted from a novel by Graham Greene, The Quiet American *questions America's involvement in Vietnam in the 1950s, with its story of a love triangle between an American aid-worker, a British journalist, and a Vietnamese woman.*

MODERN WARS

While modern warfare is greatly different from the blood-soaked battlefields of the past, contemporary films continue to expose the atrocities of war, with terrorist attacks, violent revolutions and fierce civil wars.

FREEDOM FIGHTERS

Set in the years leading up to the Vietnam wars, *Indochine* (1992) examines the upheaval in Vietnam, as the colony struggles for independence from France. *The Killing Fields* (1984) looks at Cambodia's civil war, as an American reporter witnesses the rise to power of the murderous Khmer Rouge, the **communist** regime which killed over a million of its own people. On the other hand, *Gandhi* (1982) is a **pacifist** film with no violence, depicting India's peaceful struggle for independence.

THE BATTLE OF ALGIERS (1965)

Without a single shot of real footage, The Battle of Algiers gives a frighteningly realistic depiction of Algeria's war of independence against France. Examining one of the bloodiest revolutions in history, the film gives a balanced portrait of street fighting, torture and terrorist bombings.

WELCOME TO SARAJEVO (1997)

Using real footage, Michael Winterbottom's film Welcome to Sarajevo *depicts a city under siege, as journalists try to shake up the West to the atrocities of the Bosnian War with images of ordinary people being executed and villages burnt down.*

GILLO PONTECORVO

After a short career as a journalist, Italian filmmaker Gillo Pontecorvo started directing documentaries in the 1950s. Following his Oscar-nominated film Kapò *(1959) about a Nazi concentration camp, Pontecorvo directed* The Battle of Algiers *(1965) as well as* Burn! *(1969) and* Operation Ogre *(1980), about the Basque people's fight for independence in Spain.*

THREE KINGS (1999)

This film is set in the final days of the Gulf War and follows four American soldiers in search of hidden Iraqi gold stolen from Kuwait. Instead they discover Iraqi freedom fighters encouraged by the United States to revolt, who have now been abandoned and face execution. Combining brutal torture and dark comedy, this is an unconventional war film.

IN THE COMBAT ZONE

With wars raging all over the world, modern war films often examine the role of international aid in foreign conflicts. While *Welcome to Sarajevo* (1997) questions why war is ignored by other countries, the black comedy *No Man's Land* (2001) examines the role of United Nations peacekeeping forces, as they fail to help a wounded man stuck on a mine. *Tears of the Sun* (2003) focuses on a civil war in Nigeria, as soldiers protect a group of refugees.

BLACK HAWK DOWN (2001)

Set in the frontlines of the Battle of Mogadishu, Ridley Scott's Black Hawk Down *follows a platoon of U.S. rangers. Their mission – to rescue men left on the ground after two Black Hawk helicopters have crashed. Then they have to fight their way out of the city.*

FILM TECHNOLOGY

THE ART OF MATTE PAINTING

From Gone with the Wind *(1939) to* Titanic *(1997), matte paintings have been a cheap and easy way to create the illusion of expensive, epic sets. Combining real footage of live actors with scenery painted on glass, the matte painting was one of the first special effects. To create the illusion of a spectacular background, a sheet of glass painted with scenery is placed between the camera and the live actors, who perform on a small set.*

BRUSH STROKES

With a hole in the painting to film live action, the real set is matched to the glass scenery, through careful positioning and special lighting. Mechanical miniatures can be used in the same way to create the impression of a moving background.

COMBINING IMAGES

Another way to combine live action with artificial scenery is to project real footage into the background by projecting on to a screen behind the actors. This is often used to create moving backgrounds in car scenes. Front projection creates sharper scenery by projecting on to a screen from a mirror in front of the actor. Latent image projection combines the image by using the film twice, once filming the background with the real set blacked out and once filming the actors.

GLOSSARY

cinematography

art of photography and camera work in films

Cold War

state of hostility between nations without an actual war. The term usually describes the situation between the Soviet Union and the United States between 1945 and 1991.

communism

political theory that social class should be abolished and all land and wealth that a country has should be shared out equally

Cultural Revolution

period of political upheaval in China in 1966–1968

Dark Ages

period in Europe between the fall of the Roman Empire and the Middle Ages, c.500–1100. It was seen as a time when culture and learning were in decline.

genre

style or category of film, art or literature

Holocaust

mass murder of Jews under the German Nazi regime in World War II

Ku Klux Klan

secret organization of white people in the United States who are violently opposed to black people

moors

members of a north west African Muslim people

no man's land

area between two opposing armies that is not controlled by either

pacifism

belief that disputes should be settled peacefully and that war and violence are always wrong

patriotism

term that describes love or devotion to your country

propaganda

information that is often biased or misleading and used to promote a political cause or point of view

Roman Empire

empire under Roman rule established in 27 BC

INDEX